Becoming Israel:

Jacob's Struggle

JACQUIE HOEKSTRA

Second Edition

GLORY PEAK PUBLISHING

Brownsville, Oregon

ISBN: 979-8-9909035-6-2 (sc)
ISBN: 979-8-9909035-7-9 (e)

 GLORY PEAK
PUBLISHING

jacquiehoekstra.com

Book cover design by Matt and Anne Spaanem

Glory Peak Publishing rev. date: 03/17/2025

Dedication

To Milton and Barbara Atkisson for taking me to the Billy Graham Crusade in Portland, Oregon, in 1992; for giving me my first Bible, a dusty rose Thompson Chain-Reference Bible; for taking me to your church; for paying my way to my first women's retreat; and for introducing me to Bible Study Fellowship. I asked Jesus to send someone to show me the way, and He sent me you. I am eternally grateful and forever changed by your "yes."

Contents

Introduction

Becoming Israel is a five-week study of Jacob's early life, marriages, children, and how and when his name changed to Israel. The five daily lessons per week follow Jacob from when his father, Isaac, prayed for his wife, Rebekah, to conceive until he returned to Canaan with the name for which his descendants are known, Israel.

Looking at his early life and parents will reveal insights into his character. Then, it will be shown how the God of Abraham and Isaac also became the God of Jacob. Through this journey, you will meet Jacob's parents, Isaac and Rebekah; his brother, Esau; his uncle, Laban; his wives, Leah and Rachel; and his children. While the study will touch on his relationship with his sons, this subject is too broad for study.

There are a few unanswerable questions in this study. They are meant to pique curiosity and provide for lively discussion. If studying in a group, you do not all have to agree on these answers. Take time to self-reflect and consider why you lean toward the direction you do. What does it say about you or to you? Do additional study to see if the Bible gives you further insight and whether it changes or solidifies your stance. We can wrestle with our theology like Jacob wrestled with his. Who knows what God will reveal to us as we lean into Him and search for truth?

The best way to approach any Bible study is to imagine everything you know about the section scripture written on a slate in your mind. Then, imagine erasing it all before you begin your study. If you come to scripture with a blank slate, scriptures come alive with revelation. Nuggets of truth you have never noticed will jump off the page. We can pass over the new thing God wants to reveal when we come with what we already know. You can then combine what you have known and learned to gain a broader understanding of the text.

Jesus told His disciples, "When He, the Spirit of truth, has come, He will guide you into all truth" (John 16:13). Pray and ask God to give you eyes to see, ears to hear, and a heart to receive. Trust Him to be true to His word and expect to receive new insights. Most of all, enjoy the journey because this is about spending time with the living God, not merely finding the right answers. We are looking for the God-answers. Seek Him, and He will be found by you (Jeremiah 29:13).

JOY IN THE JOURNEY.

Leaving Canaan

Read: Genesis 25:19-28

1. What did Isaac pray for, and how did God answer?

2. What sent Rebekah to prayer?

3. What information did the Lord give Rebekah concerning the twins?

4. What circumstance earned Jacob his name? What does his name mean?

5.   What kind of men were Jacob and Esau?

6.   What do we learn about their relationships with their parents? How did this influence their character development?

7.   How does your upbringing compare and contrast with Jacob and Esau's? How does your upbringing affect you now?

Day Two—Siblings

Read: Genesis 25:29-34

8. What were Jacob and Esau both doing?

9. What did Esau ask for, and what was Jacob's condition? What was Jacob asking for?

10. What does this say about Jacob? How did his action relate to the promise spoken to his mother?

11. A saying is, "God helps those who help themselves." Is this biblical? (Give scripture reference(s) to support your position.)

12. How did Esau treat his birthright? What might be his reason for treating it as he did?

13. What did you learn about Jacob in this section of scripture?

Day Three—Favored Sons
Read Genesis 27:1-40

14. What did Isaac want to do for his eldest son, Esau?

15. Who was listening, and what was her response? Why might this have been her response?

16. Was Jacob comfortable with his mother's plan? What was his worry, and how was he put at ease?

17. Did they get what they wanted? Was this what the Lord promised Rebekah?

18. How might God have provided all this for Jacob without Jacob's help? Did Jacob help or hinder God's plan and promise?

19. How are you trusting God to fulfill His promises to you today? How do you get past the desire to help?

Day Four—Effects of Favoritism

Read: Genesis 27:41-28:5

20. How did Esau feel about Jacob after this? What plan did he make?

21. What plan did Rebekah suggest to spare her favored son? How long did she expect it to take?

22. What did Isaac do when he called Jacob back to him? Why do you think he responded this way?

23. What was Isaac's charge to Jacob? With what blessing did he bless him this time?

DAY FIVE—JACOB LEAVES CANAAN

GENESIS 28:10-22

24. Consider what we've learned about Jacob so far. How do you think he might have been feeling as he laid his head on the rock?

25. What promises did Jacob receive as he slept? Why do you think God approached him at this time?

26. What was Jacob's immediate response? How could he not have known before?

27. Write a time when God revealed Himself to you in a way you had not known Him before.

28. How did the experience change him? What was his vow?

29. How does your story compare or contrast with Jacob's?

30. Write your story in the space below. Tell of how you met Jesus and how meeting Him has changed your life and/or how you are seeking Him in this season.

Marriage Contracts

When the boys were struggling inside her womb, Rebekah sought the Lord. He affirmed to her that the older would serve the younger. This could be why she favored Jacob, the younger son. Rebekah and Jacob both worked to fulfill the promise God gave to her before the twins were born. They moved in their own strength and their own power. They tricked, schemed, and deceived to get what God had promised. After all, "God helps those who help themselves," right? No. This quote is attributed to Benjamin Franklin. God's Word teaches us to "trust in the Lord with all your heart, and lean not on your own understanding; in all your ways acknowledge Him, and He shall direct your paths. Do not be wise in your own eyes; fear the Lord and depart from evil" (Proverbs 3:5-7).

Jacob's parents sent him to Padan Aram to find his Uncle Laban and marry one of his daughters. We know Jacob was a homebody. Esau was the man's man, and Jacob was the mama's boy. He was gentle and stayed in tents, which meant he was probably a shepherd. He would travel with the flock to find food and water for them. Jacob most likely dwelt in tents away from home with the flocks when Esau came upon him and his lentil stew. This explains why Esau did not just go to his parents for help when Jacob sought his birthright.

Jacob and Rebekah's actions tore their family apart. In the end, it separated mother and son forever. While she thought it would only take a few days, plus the two-month round trip, Jacob was gone for twenty years. Rebekah died before he made his way back to her. Her attempt to help God fulfill His promise cost her more than she could have imagined. It cost her relationship with her favored son for the rest of her life. However, it did not cost Jacob the promises because God is faithful even when we are not (2 Timothy 2:13). Their unwillingness to wait for His timing did them damage, but God was and is able to set things right (Romans 8:28).

Jacob went with a verbal blessing and nothing more. He journeyed to find a bride with no gift to offer. The customary practice in the East was for the groom's father to seek a bride for his son. Then, the fathers would negotiate a contract between themselves. They were looking for a good match for their children and a mutually beneficial relationship. The groom's side would then give a gift to the bride's family, and the bride's father would provide her with a dowry that would pass to the groom once they were married.[i] Let's begin with an example of a marriage contract, which helps us know Jacob's mother and uncle better before we catch up with Jacob again in Padan Aram.

Day One—A Wife for Isaac

Read: Genesis 24:1-31

Abraham sent his servant to find a wife for his son Isaac. The servant would stand in proxy to conduct a marriage contract on behalf of his master, Abraham.

1. Where did Abraham's servant meet Rebekah, and how did he know she was the one?

2. What did the servant do when Rebekah finished watering the camels? How did she respond?

3. Who ran to the well to meet Abraham's servant? What prompted him to run to meet him?

4. How did he greet the servant at the well? Why do you think he greeted him this way?

Day Two—Business First

Read: Genesis 24:32-61

5.   What was the servant more eager to do than eat?

6.   How did Laban and Bethuel respond to his proposal? Why might Laban have been so involved if marriage contracts were traditionally negotiated between fathers?

7.   What did Abraham's servant do when they accepted his proposal?

8.   Who tried to keep them from leaving? Why do you think they did this?

9.   What was the wise servant's response?

10. Have you ever experienced a good reason to delay what the Lord has given you to do? How did you respond? What did you learn from this experience?

Day Three—Jacob Meets Rachel

Read: Genesis 24:11-31, 29:1-19

11. Compare and contrast Jacob's meeting Rachel with Abraham's servant's meeting Rebekah. (Genesis 24:11-31; 29:1-13)

Servant's Experience	Jacob's Experience

12. What was behind Jacob's suggestion the men should water their sheep and leave?

Day Four—Jacob Meets Laban

Read: Genesis 29:13-14

13. Why do you think Laban ran to the well to greet Jacob? What do you think his expectations were? Explain your answer.

14. What did Jacob share with his uncle? Why do you think he did this? Do you think this was wise?

15. What was Laban's response after hearing Jacob's woes and reasons for fleeing his home? What was he saying?

Day Five—Uncle Laban's Contract
Read: Genesis 29:15-19

Jacob had no obligation to work for Laban as a hired man. As his nephew, Jacob's work should have been enough to earn him room and board at his uncle's place.ⁱⁱ

16. Why might Laban have sought to secure a contract with Jacob? What advantages did Laban perceive he had over Jacob?

17. What kind of a contract did Jacob seek to enter with Laban?

18. How were the sisters described?

The bride price was customarily thirty or forty shekels of silver. A shepherd's annual wages were approximately ten silver shekels.ⁱⁱⁱ

19. Why would Jacob offer such a high price for his groom's gift? Does this speak to why the groom usually did not get involved in the marriage contract?

20. Do you think Jacob was in a position to make a good match for himself and his family? Why or why not?

21. What lesson(s) do you get from the following Bible characters? How can you apply them to your own life?

Abraham's Servant –

Laban –

Jacob –

22. What lessons will you apply to your life this week?

Wives and Children

We come to this week's study with an understanding of Jacob and Laban's characters. Jacob's early life in Canaan and his uncle's shrewd contract negotiations reveal the men. Jacob seems to transfer his trust and affection for his mother onto her brother, Laban. Jacob's month-long journey to find his uncle depleted his resources. He was out on his own and on a mission to find his wife. Meeting the very beautiful Rachel at the well, a story similar to his mother's betrothal may have moved him. His relief at finding Laban at last and seeing Laban's possessions and beautiful daughter left him defenseless. He told Laban everything. He seemed to assume Laban would love him like his mother loved him. He was wrong. We will see just how wrong in today's lesson.

Jacob's love for Rachel began with a vision—the vision of her beauty. The Bible says, "Leah's eyes were delicate, but Rachel was beautiful of form and appearance" (Genesis 29:17). Some believe this means there was something wrong with Leah's eyes. However, studying the terms, we find this was not a derogatory comment. Maybe it could be said this way: Leah was pleasant, but Rachel was drop-dead gorgeous! Maybe Leah had a good face, but Rachel had the whole package. [iv]

With no gift to offer for Rachel, Jacob pledged himself as an indentured servant for three to four years longer than necessary to prove his love and show his high esteem for her.[v] We know a father or his emissary conducted the contract for the couple. This is a good example of why. A suitor seeking to impress would make a bad deal for himself based on pride and emotion. The unbiased party would not only make a good deal but a good match. By the wording, it seems Jacob was enamored with Rachel because of her appearance. There is no way to know their suitability for one another in one month's time.

It was customary for the older daughter to marry first—a practice continuing today in many parts of the East. Jacob would not have been uninformed in this matter. Maybe he offered the extra gift of service to make up for side-stepping Leah. A couple of reasons exist for this custom. One was to not shame the older sister, who might not be as physically appealing as the younger. Another reason was to keep the family from being indefinitely burdened with her financial care. Daughters were a means of economic gain and position in society.[vi] An unmarried daughter was a financial burden and a disgrace for the family. Jacob and Laban both knew this when they made their deal.

Polygamy was uncommon in their culture. The only time polygamy was accepted was when the wife was barren, as seen in Abraham and Sarah's story.[vii] A servant-wife or concubine would be given to the husband by the barren wife because the primary purpose of marriage was to produce an heir. The servant would act as a surrogate for the free wife. Children born to her would be considered the children of the free wife. [viii]

DAY ONE—JACOB

READ: GENESIS 29:20-30

1. What is said of Jacob's love for Rachel?

2. Who sought the conclusion of the contract? Why do you think he was the one to approach the subject?

3. How was the request responded to? How did this make things appear?

4. What went wrong according to the contract? How do you think it was pulled off?

5. When did Jacob discover the switch, and how did he react? How could he not have noticed before?

Day Two—Leah

Read: Genesis 29:21-30

6. Knowing the customs of the land, what do you think Leah thought when Jacob first came to them looking for a wife?

7. How do you think Leah felt for the seven years her younger sister was betrothed to Jacob? (Consider how she may have been treated in her community.)

8. Have you ever felt passed over? What did you do about it? What should you do about it?

9. Consider and describe Leah's experience the following morning as Jacob reacts to his discovery of her in his bed.

10. How did Laban respond to Jacob's complaint? Do you think this was his plan the whole time?

11. Why do you think Jacob went along with it?

12. Why do you think he kept the one he did not contract for?

13. Do you think Leah had a choice whether or not to deceive Jacob? Either way, what do you think her expectations were for the future?

14. How did things work out for Leah? Did she get what she deserved, or was she the victim of two cheaters?

15. Who do you think was God's chosen wife for Jacob?

DAY THREE—FIRST WIFE SECOND CLASS
READ: GENESIS 29:31-30:1

Why might a barren wife be compelled to give her husband a servant-wife to bear an heir for her? A barren wife risked losing her position in the arranged family. She could be given a lower position as another wife was taken, she could be detested, or worse, she could be returned to her relatives.[ix] The heir was important to their culture in carrying on the family holdings and social status. They needed an heir to carry on the family's affairs and care for them when they were old. They carried on the family line and brought social status to the family.[x]

The birthright belonged to the eldest son. He would inherit a double portion of his father's holdings. If there were five brothers, the estate would be divided into six portions, and the eldest son would receive two portions. He would become the head and priest of the family and inherit the covenant promises.[xi] Firstborn status was not affected by the status of the mother. Whether the first-born son was born to the free wife, the preferred wife, or the slave, it did not matter. The only time the father could disinherit a firstborn son was when the child was born to a slave, and he did not acknowledge the child. He would be required to grant the woman and her son their freedom.[xii] The story of Hagar and Ishmael is an example of this (Gen. 21:9-14).

Another important part of bearing children was naming them. The name could be associated with something the child did at birth or something going on in the world when the child was born. The name could often be linked by wordplay. Jacob's name does not mean heel, literally. It is a word that sounds like heel. However, the name did carry an expectation regarding how the child's life would transpire. It would also increase in meaning and significance as the child grew and matured.[xiii] Jacob, for example, began his life by grasping his brother's heel, then taking his birthright, and then his blessing. Jacob's descendants would later take the Promised Land. Both began with a struggle; then both grew into something else.

16. How did God bless Leah? Why was this significant? Why do you think Rachel was not yet granted children?

17. List the names Leah gave to her first four children. Look in your Bible's notes and write what their names mean and Leah's reasons for choosing each name.

18. What do you learn about Leah's relationship with Jacob's God? What do you learn about her heart's desire?

19. What would Jacob have heard in their children's names? How do you think the names affected him? Why?

20. What significance do Leah's sons Levi and Judah hold in history?

Day Four—Second Wife First Class

Read: Genesis 30:1-8

21. From what we have read so far, describe what Rachel's life might have been like in her father's house when she met Jacob and for the seven years she was betrothed to Jacob. What might her relationship with her older sister have been like?

22. Imagine and describe what it must have been like for her to have her father replace her with her sister on her wedding night.

23. What emotion did Rachel express toward her sister, Leah?

24. How did Rachel respond to Jacob over her barrenness? What do you think she feared?

25. How did Jacob respond to Rachel? Does this reveal anything about Rachel's relationship with Jacob's God?

26. What was Rachel's solution to her barrenness? What was the result?

27. List the names Rachel gave her children and their meanings.

28. Who did Rachel credit with the births of her sons? What does this reveal about Rachel at this point in her life?

DAY FIVE—SISTER WIVES

READ: GENESIS 30:9-24

29. How did Leah respond to Rachel's maid having children? Why do you think she did this?

30. What did Leah name her two children by her maid, and what did their names mean? Did she credit God with their births? What does this reveal about her?

31. How did the struggle between the sister wives affect Reuben? What interest did he have in their dealings?

32. Leah bore Jacob two more sons. What did she name them, and what did their names mean? What do their names tell us about Leah at this point in her life?

33. What was repaired with the birth of her sixth son?

34. What happened for Rachel once Leah made peace with her position? Why do you think it happened this way?

35. What was repaired with the birth of her first son?

36. What more do we learn about Rachel in the birth and naming of her firstborn and Jacob's eleventh son?

Going Home

Jacob left his mother and father to find a wife at his uncle Laban's house and return after a few days, just like Abraham's servant had done with his mother, Rebekah. In this section of scripture, we catch up with Jacob after two seven-year contracts, four wives, and eleven children. His uncle cheated him and coerced him to marry both of his daughters. Laban's plan was most likely to dump his less attractive daughter, Leah, on the first guy he could trick into marrying her. Laban had the power of both men and resources. Jacob had little choice but to give in to his uncle's schemes. His own scheming, which had gotten him there, left him with no means to empower him.

Leah probably saw Jacob as the great hope of getting free from her father's grip and out from under her younger sister's shadow. Her name rightfully means weary. Leah must have been weary of her living situation with no suitor or even the prospect of one to come. Weary of men coming to seek a wife, preferring the younger, and passing on both, since they had to marry the elder first.

Jacob showed up for the same reason: to find a wife. She was, by custom, his only option. What a spark of hope she must have felt when she saw him. Yes, she probably expected him to be smitten with her younger sister, but he could not have her. He had to marry her. It was just the way things were. She knew he would learn to love her. That is how arranged marriages work; the couple learns to love one another —well, most of the time, anyway. It could work out for them, too.

How devastated Leah must have been when her father betrayed her and contracted for the younger. How betrayed she must have felt by Jacob to do such a thing. She would have carried the shame for seven years while he worked out his contract. She would hear the whispers; she would feel them, too. What was being done was not right, but what could she do? She was a daughter who brought no prosperity to a family greedy for affluence and status. She was as much or more Laban's property as she was his daughter. She had no rights and could not defy her father lest she be cast out.

We don't know what transpired between Laban and Leah the night she replaced Rachel in the wedding chamber. Was she complicit, or was she forced to deceive? Maybe it was a little of both. Maybe her trickster father assured her he realized his wrong and knew she was the rightful bride. The younger should not have been given before the older. He would rectify the mistake. Maybe he convinced her Jacob did wrong; therefore, tricking him was okay.

Or, maybe, in anger, she stepped into agreement, believing it to be her rightful position. Maybe she thought that once Jacob saw the error of his ways, he would settle with her and live in perpetual happiness. Most likely, regardless of heart longings and motives, Leah had no choice but to obey her father's will. One thing is relatively sure. She most likely did not expect her father to trap her in a polygamist marriage with her sister. She could not have agreed to go from second-class daughter to second-class wife. It is more likely she was fooled or forced, but with the belief that she had finally beaten her sister at something. We really can't know because the Bible does not make this clear.

Leah seemed to have a relationship with Jacob's God from the beginning of their relationship. It is seen through the names she chose for her children. She bore six of his eleven sons in Haran, two being the ancestors of the priests and kings of Israel and, ultimately, the Messiah. We see God's blessing on her life regardless of her station in life. God waited to give Rachel children until Leah found her place of contentment. He may also have been waiting for Rachel to grow in faith. We see the sister-wives struggle with one another as Jacob and Esau struggled. Leah bore Jacob's firstborn and rightful heir. However, Jacob would deny Reuben's position for the child of the favored wife. Leah's sons grew up, half of the nation of Israel, somewhat disdained by their father, or maybe it just felt that way. He kept them, but they all fell into second place behind Joseph, the favored wife's son. This is Jacob's becoming Israel. God uses fallible human beings to fulfill His infallible plan.

Day One—A New Contract

READ: GENESIS 30:25-43

1. What did Jacob want to do after Joseph was born? Why do you think he wanted to do it then?

2. How did Laban respond to Jacob's request?

3. What did Jacob contract for, and why? Why might Laban have jumped at Jacob's offer?

4. What did Jacob say would answer for him? When did he say it would answer for him? How long is that in your experience?

5. What does Jacob's technique in caring for the flocks reveal about him?

6. How did it work out for him? To whom does the credit belong?

DAY TWO—BREAKING FREE

READ: GENESIS 31:1-21

7. Why did Jacob decide to leave his Uncle Laban's home and return to his own land? What promise did he receive?

8. Who did he consult with before leaving? Why both of them? What does this say about the relationships at this time?

9. How did they respond to Jacob's proposal? Why?

10. How did they travel, and how did they leave? Why do you think they left this way?

11. How had God been active in Jacob's life? (See verses 3-13)

DAY THREE—POWER TRANSFER
READ: GENESIS 31:22-55

Household gods were generally connected to good fortune and fertility.[xiv]

12. Why was Laban unable to harm Jacob when he caught up to him? What did he do instead?

13. Who had his idols? What does this say about this person's character and relationship with Jacob's God? Why might they have taken them?

14. When did Jacob find the courage to rebuke his uncle? What did Jacob say it was like to work for Laban?

15. What did Laban seek once he lost the upper hand? Did he get it? What happened after that?

DAY FOUR—BECOMING ISRAEL

READ: GENESIS 32:1-13 (28:12-22)

16. Why do you think the angels of God appeared to Jacob as he continued his journey home?

17. What message did Jacob send with his men to Esau? What was he saying?

18. What report did they bring back to Jacob? How did he take the news?

19. What was Jacob's next move to prepare for meeting Esau? Why did he do this?

Day Five—Jacob's Prayer

Read: Genesis 32:9-12

20. Once Jacob had done all he knew to do, what did he do next?

21. To Whom did Jacob pray?

22. Of what did Jacob remind Him? Why do you think he did this?

23. Have you ever prayed, reminding God of His promises? Why might this be a good practice?

24. What had God shown Jacob, and how did it make him feel?

25. Share a time you felt the same way Jacob did.

26. What had God done for Jacob? Was this His promise fulfilled?

27. For what did Jacob ask?

28. What did Jacob remind God He said?

29. Tell of a time you took steps of obedience and prayed a prayer like this.

Family Reunion

Day One—Jacob's Gift
Read: Genesis 32:13-20

Jacob's livestock was his livelihood.

1. How did Jacob choose his gift for Esau? Was this an act of faith or contrition?

2. What was the total gift Jacob sent to Esau? (Be specific.) How easy would it be for you to do the same?

3.   How did Jacob deliver his gift to Esau?

4.   What did he command his servants to say? How many droves were there?

5.   What was Jacob's motive for the present to Esau?

6.   What message might Esau have received?

Day Two—Jacob's Wrestling Match
Read: Genesis 32:21-32
Jacob sent the droves with word he was coming after them.

7.   According to verse 21, what did he do? Did he lie?

8.   What did Jacob do with his family and their procession? Where did that leave Jacob?

9.   What happened when Jacob was left alone?

10. What did the Man do when he could not prevail?

11. Did this work for Him? How do you know?

12. What was Jacob's condition for letting Him go?

13. Do you think Jacob knew Who he was wrestling with?

14. Tell of a time you held on through the pain to get to the blessing.

15. How did the Man bless him?

16. What was His reason for this name? What does this mean to you?

17. For what information did Jacob ask, and what response did he receive?

18. What did Jacob name the place?

19. How did this experience prepare Jacob to enter the Promised Land?

20. Have you entered the Promised Land through a personal experience with Jesus? Write down the experience.

DAY THREE—A CHANGED MAN

READ: GENESIS 32:31-33:4

21. Jacob was awake all night, literally wrestling with God. What shape was he in as he crossed over at sunrise?

22. What Israeli tradition was born from this event?

23. Jacob, the changed man, crossed over at dawn, and what did he see?

24. What action did Jacob take upon this sight? Was this old nature at work? Why or why not?

25. How did Jacob line his family up to meet Esau? List them out in order with their children.

26. What message does this lineup give to Jacob's wives, children, and onlookers?

27. How have you experienced this in your own life? How has this affected you? How has Jesus made a difference?

DAY FOUR—TWINS REUNITED

READ: GENESIS 33:3-11

28. Leah's second-class status actually allowed her some firsts. What first experiences do you see here for Leah? What does this say to you when you are overlooked?

29. Where did Jacob line himself up? What does this reveal about his character?

30. How did Jacob present himself to Esau? Why so much? What did this say to Esau? What does it say about Jacob?

31. How did Esau greet his brother? Does this surprise you? Why or why not?

32. What did Jacob say of his wives and children? What might the old Jacob have said?

33. How did Esau react to Jacob's gift?

34. Why did Jacob urge Esau to take his gift? What purpose did it serve?

35. What convinced Esau to receive Jacob's gift?

Day Five—Jacob Settles
Read: Genesis 33:12-20

36. What was Esau's suggestion?

37. Why did Jacob decline?

38. What more did Esau offer? Why the persistence?

39. Where did Jacob finally settle?

40. What was the first thing Jacob did after he bought a parcel of land? What does this tell you about Jacob?

41. Write a statement about Jacob's life. How does it compare or contrast with your life?

Appendix

AUTHOR NOTES

Congratulations on completing this journey with Jacob as he became Israel. I hope you have seen a few of these Bible characters in a new light and drawn closer to God in the process. If you enjoyed this study and would like others to know, please consider leaving your review at your favorite online bookstore. I thank you in advance.

ACKNOWLEDGMENTS

I want to take a moment to thank all those who have supported and helped me along this journey with Jacob. Without these wonderful people, this part of my journey would have never unfolded. I am eternally grateful to my husband, Martin, who has always supported "whatever the Lord tells [me] to do." He is truly God's chosen for me. He always believes in me and encourages me to reach farther than I think I can go. Thank you, Martin.

I married into a good family. The following person I want to thank is Cynthia Overson, my sister-in-love and editor. Cynthia, thank you for your heart in pouring over my work with diligence and honest critique.

I also want to thank those who took the time to do the study and gave me helpful and quality feedback. I am forever grateful for the care you have shown me by giving your time and effort to bless me in such a way. I am humbled.

Lesly Ezelle, my beloved British-born friend, elder, mentor, and opera-going partner. Your constant grace, wisdom, and encouragement have strengthened and challenged my walk with Christ. Karen Hamilton, I watch your life with Christ and your heart to serve, making me want to be more and better than I am. Ann Jendro, I appreciate all you do to serve, in love, those around you. Kathy Kelly, you are a welcome addition to our Bible study groups, women's ministries, and church. Pat McClanahan, you are a treasure. Your heart to serve is beautiful to behold. Lorraine O'Neal, you spoke life into my walk with Christ when others did the opposite. Kay Ritter, you are a prayer warrior and a joy of a person to share this space and time with. Linda Romig, you are a gentle and kind soul. Devon Stone, I'm so glad our paths have crossed. You are a treasure to me. Tracy Van Wyk, my Dutch sister in Christ, you have such a beautiful heart for the Lord. Suzi Shoemaker, I'm so glad the Lord brought us together. I appreciate your honest critique and your fierce loyalty to friends and family.

You have helped me produce this Bible study, and each of you has impacted my life in unique and special ways. I feel the love, and I hope you know you also have my heart.

Jacquie Hoekstra has authored three highly rated Bible studies, including Peter: A Life Transformed, Becoming Israel: Jacob's Struggle, and Nehemiah Build That Wall. She has also published a short story, This Servant's Hands. Her passion is teaching the Word, recognizing and calling out gifts in others, and releasing them to fulfill their purposes.

Jacquie's thirty years of experience in leading groups, Bible studies, and ministry shine through her written works. She teaches with humor and authenticity. Her journey with inner healing and overcoming trials makes her studies relatable.

Jacquie has degrees in Bible study from Life Pacific College and Theology from Canyon College. She was ordained by The International Church of the Foursquare Gospel in 2008. However, she no longer holds credentials due to a couple of moves for her husband's work and no longer having a specific appointment. She continues to serve through preaching, teaching, and serving on her church's inner healing team.

Jacquie's last move placed her in Brownsville, Oregon, a small historic town in the Willamette Valley. Brownsville is famous for two things. The movie Stand By Me was filmed there, and it is in the grass-seed capital of the world. Jacquie enjoys the ever-changing views of the farmlands and watching lambs and calves frolic in the fields. She often spies Bald Eagles and other birds of prey. The air is fresh, and the pace of life is peaceful.

Jacquie and her husband enjoy their home in the foothills of the Cascade Mountains. They have a westerly view of the valley, grass-seed and hazelnut tree farms, and the Coast Range Mountains in the background. Jacquie especially enjoys watching and photographing sunsets and thanks God daily for the blessings.

ENDNOTES

i   Vos, H. F. (1999). *New Illustrated Bible Manners & Customs*. Nashville: Thomas Nelson Publishers, p. 38.

ii   Walton, J. H. (1997). *The IVP Bible Background Commentary Old Testament*. Downers Grove: IL., p. 62.

iii   Keil, C. F. (2011). *Commentary on the Old Testament Volume 1 The Pentateuch*. Edinburgh: T. &. T. Clark., p. 183.

iv   Walton, *IVPOT*, p. 61.

v   Vos, *NIBMC*, p. 30.

vi   Walton, *IVPOT*, p. 62.

vii   Vos, *NIBMC*, p.17.

viii   Vos, *NIBMC*, p. 39.

ix   Walton, *IVPOT*, p. 62.

x   Vos, *NIBMC*, p.39.

xi   Vos, *NIBMC*, p. 40.

xii   Vos, *NIBMC*, p. 42

xiii   Walton, *IVPOT*, p. 58.

xiv   Vos, *NIBMC*, p. 41.